C000220649

Harrison's Warwickshire

A Collection of Photographs of the County by

William Jerome Harrison FGS

with an Introduction by Peter James

Birmingham Books and Warwickshire Books, 1992

Harrison's Warwickshire

A Collection of Photographs of the County by William Jerome Harrison FGS

Published jointly by Birmingham Books and Warwickshire Books, 1992

First edition, December 1992

Copyright © Birmingham Books and Warwickshire Books, 1992

Designed and typeset by Carnegie Publishing, 18 Maynard St., Preston, Lancs.
Printed in the UK by The Bath Press, Bath, Avon

British Library Cataloguing-in-Publication Data
A CIP catalogue record for this book is available from the British Library

ISBN (case)   1-871942-08-X
ISBN (pbk)   1-871942-09-8

Introduction

by Peter James

The shire is chipped and chopped from one year to another by speculative builders and restorers, and Time; old landmarks pass away, interesting half-timbered houses crumble, and are replaced by stucco and galvanised roofs; dainty old villages, once pretty as a poem, with their quaint gables and windows and thatches are becoming trim, ugly and civilised; the agricultural labourers shave in the modern manner, and the new generation of mothers ape the fashions of their betters instead of maintaining the becoming costumes of two centuries ago and in a little while Warwickshire will have put off its poetry and put on the airs and graces of the big towns . . . Photographers . . . cannot stop these things; what they can do is to make a picture of Warwickshire as it is today in order that future students and historians . . . may see all that remains of the architecture of the early ages, all the 'sermons in stone' that are still to be read, all the features and characters of the shire that are of interest and value.

'Photographers' Jaunts: A Day Out With The Warwickshire Survey', *The Birmingham Daily Gazette*, 10 June 1891.

From the dawn of the photographic era to the present day, the belief that the optical and chemical processes of photography produced pictures of 'absolute truthfulness and reliable authenticity', has led to the widespread use of the camera as a means of preserving historical records. In the first fifty years of its history, the technical complexities and high costs of operating early photographic processes meant that access to the medium was restricted to a relatively small number of wealthy, educated amateurs and a larger number of professional photographers, who dictated the style and content of early photographic records. In the late 1870s, the introduction of simpler, cheaper photographic technologies made photography, and therefore photographic record making, accessible to a wide range of people for the first time in its history. In 1881 William Jerome Harrison purchased his first camera and joined with thousands of others in this 'amateur photographic revolution'.

The forces of progress, born of the industrial revolution, which brought about the 'democratisation' of photography, also had a substantial impact on the physical and social landscape of Warwickshire in the late nineteenth century. The effects of industrialisation and urbanisation stirred fears among some commentators that Warwickshire would soon change beyond all recognition. Prompted, in part, by such concerns, Harrison set out to make a photographic record of the county for the benefit of posterity.

Little is known of Harrison's early photographic career, for sadly no negatives or prints appear to have survived from this period. However, it is clear from the many articles that he subsequently wrote on the subject that Harrison recognised photography as a 'New Power', and believed it was 'the task of photographers – and more especially amateurs – to show of what infinite applications, and those of the highest and most accurate nature, photography' was capable.

In 1884, Harrison joined with other local photographers, both amateur and professional, to form the Birmingham Photographic Society (BPS). Shortly after its formation, a number of members confessed that they were unsure how best to expend their photographic energies. Harrison responded with a paper entitled 'On the Work of a Local Photographic Society', in which he emphasised that:

Much useful local work may be done by a local photographic society. By securing accurate representations of old buildings we can furnish a record for posterity, whose accuracy cannot be disputed, and whose interest in the future would be great. But I would not only photograph the old buildings – I would secure on rapid plates impressions of the daily appearance of our streets, of the principal lines of thoroughfare, and of the busy crowds by which they are traversed.

This paper marked the beginnings of what was to become a life-long involvement with photographic record making.

Although Harrison's proposals were not taken up immediately by the BPS, the idea of survey photography, as it became known, began to take off elsewhere and the first accounts of co-ordinated photographic surveys by amateur photographers appeared in the photographic periodicals around 1888. Harrison, by this time a familiar name in British and American photographic journals, continually encouraged his fellow photographers to apply themselves to survey work. These efforts were eventually rewarded, for he noted a 'growing desire among the English photographic societies to make themselves of real service to the community'. Encouraged by these developments, Harrison sketched out a plan for obtaining a 'complete photographic record' of the district surrounding the BPS headquarters in early 1889. By October that year, he transformed this draft into a detailed plan: 'Some Notes on a Proposed Photographic Survey of Warwickshire', which he presented to members of the Vesey Club, a scientific and philosophical society in Sutton Coldfield. Harrison's proposal gained the wholehearted support of John Benjamin

Stone – later to be come Sir Benjamin Stone – a local industrialist and politician who had collected 'history' and record photographs since about 1864. Like Harrison, Stone had become a photographer during the amateur revolution of the early 1880s. He was elected president of the BPS in late 1889, and in December that year called a special meeting enabling Harrison to present his proposal formally to the BPS. Harrison's ideas were accepted by the society and the Warwickshire Photographic Survey was formally established on 8 May 1890. The Survey continued working for the next sixty-five years, interrupted only by the two world wars, amassing some 10,000 photographic records of the county.

Having successfully established the Warwickshire Photographic Survey, Harrison went on to submit proposals for a national survey in 1892, and an international survey in 1893. These laid the foundations, built upon by others, which saw the evolution of a photographic record and survey movement in Britain and Europe between about 1897 and 1910.

The systematic methods for surveying Warwickshire outlined in Harrison's paper, combining elements of fieldwork, scientific and historical research and, finally, photographic record making, give some idea of the methodology Harrison adopted in making his own records. Photographers were allotted a certain area to record, usually that contained in one quarter sheet of a six-inch map. Having studied their map and drawn up a list of the promising points, the photographers were instructed to read up on the history of any churches, ruins, or other monuments of the past included in their

area for, as Harrison declared, 'If we are to "survey" Warwickshire in earnest, we must become students as well as photographers (and to my mind this will be one great good resulting from the task)'.

Much of Harrison's own research was undertaken in Birmingham Free Library and he encouraged others to do likewise. Having completed their research, the surveyors were asked to visit the area without their cameras and walk across the district, calling perhaps at inns and farmhouses, gaining information and jotting down places and times when the light would be favourable. On their next visit, accompanied by their cameras, they secured records on glass negatives and returned home to develop and print up their day's work. It seems unlikely that many of the photographers followed these instructions to the letter, preferring, perhaps, to join one of the many congenial excursions – or 'picnics for posterity's sake' as they were dubbed – arranged by Harrison and his colleagues, when notes, transport, and refreshments were laid on for them.

Harrison's own excursions into Warwickshire, usually made by train and bicycle, took place at weekends or during holidays in the photographic season which lasted, roughly speaking, from March to September. Accompanied by colleagues from the BPS or members of his family, Harrison travelled to the four corners of the county to secure his records, taking with him a set of apparatus weighing 14lbs. This consisted of a half-plate camera fitted with turn-table and behind-the-lens-shutter; three double plate-holders with pull-out aluminium slides; a three-fold wooden tripod; a variety of lenses; a changing bag and focusing cloth; a spirit level; a focusing glass; a note book and a map of the district, all contained in a stiff carrying case.

Using this equipment, Harrison captured records of Warwickshire ranging from idyllic views of quiet country lanes to snapshots of bustling street scenes. These show the influence of both science and art, often combined in the same image. Many of Harrison's compositions reveal the influence of the picturesque tradition, handed down from painters to the early amateur photographers, and thence to commercial 'views' of photographers such as Francis Frith. In these views, Harrison carefully positioned members of his family or children from a local village to enhance pictorial effect and act as human yardsticks, indicating scale within the photograph. Time appears in many guises in Harrison's prints. A church clock gives a fixed reference to a precise moment; ghostly figures denote movement in the split second before the shutter dropped, and idyllic views of the River Avon and Blythe evoke impressions of a pre-industrial era. Elsewhere, the passage of time is marked by the interface of the old and new: telegraph poles encroach into age-old views of farmers driving sheep down country lanes; a modern post box is set into the wall of a Norman chapel, and railway cuttings reveal ancient geological strata. Ramshackle buildings with unkempt thatches, and aged cottagers standing framed in the doorway of their crumbling homes, suggest the passing of a way of life and a breed of people which would soon be found only in the photographic records that forever preserve their memory.

William Jerome Harrison was born the son of a farmer in Hemsworth, near Doncaster, Yorkshire, on 16 March, 1845. It was here, according to an obituary written in 1908, 'amidst moors, fells and dales of his native county, amidst rural scenes of the most charming beauty', that he developed early in life the 'keen love of nature which in later years became the ruling passion of his life.'

It seems that Harrison was destined to join the teaching profession. He began his education by taking classes at the Westminster Practising School between 1858 and 1863, and then commenced a course of study at the Cheltenham Training College in 1864, graduating one year later, at the age of twenty, as senior prizeman and holder of the highest obtainable government certificate. He then worked as the headmaster of a number of public elementary schools between 1866 and 1872.

In 1868 Harrison began a more specific scientific education studying for the exams of the science and art department. Within the next ten years he carried off the highest distinctions in chemistry, physics, geology, and physical geography, being a double gold medallist in these last two subjects in 1872. For four of these ten years (1873–7) he studied at the Normal College of Science in South Kensington, London, where he was taught by some of the leading scientists of the day, including Frankland, Valentin, Guthrie and Judd.

Harrison's academic skills placed him at the forefront of what was to become the first generation of professional scientists and science teachers in Britain, and, in 1872, at the comparatively young age of

twenty-seven, he was appointed chief curator at the Leicester Town Museum. Here, in addition to his many curatorial duties, he established a series of science courses and public lectures which proved both popular and successful. He also commenced what was to become a life-long study of local, regional, and glacial geology: a study which, over the years, was to gain him recognition as a geologist of national repute.

Harrison's approach to life and work – for the two, it seems, were largely inseparable – was epitomised in the engraving used to illustrate his bookplate.

LET · NATURE · BE · THY · TEACHER

WILL^M JEROME · HARRISON

William J. Harrison teaching domestic economy, Birmingham Board School, 1896.

His motto – 'Let Nature Be Thy Teacher' – drawn from Wordsworth's poem, *The Tables Turned*, guided his outlook in all things, particularly the methods he devised for teaching science. Harrison defined science as 'the art of putting questions to nature and interpreting her replies'. In Leicester this involved organising geological field trips and allowing members of the public to participate in experiments and demonstrations given during his classes. Over a number of years, he gradually evolved and refined this method which he called 'observational learning'. This contrasted strongly with the traditional practice of teaching by rote: a process which, he declared, 'reduced children to the state of machines, not thinking individuals'. Observational learning involved pupils being brought 'face to face with the facts of nature', through field trips, scientific demonstrations and illustrative aids. It was in connection with this approach to teaching that Harrison first began to use photography in the 1870s.

Most geological books of the 1870s and earlier were illustrated by engravings made from hand-drawn sketches completed in the field. However, as a contemporary pointed out, these were 'often drawn without due care', and led 'to totally inaccurate ideas' being transmitted to students. Aware of the role photography had played in recording geological data since the early 1850s, Harrison began employing photographic prints and lantern slides as teaching aids. Between 1872 and 1879, he engaged John Burton, a professional photographer from Leicester, to record geological features in the county. Twelve of Burton's albumen prints

were used to illustrate Harrison's *Sketch of the Geology of Leicester and Rutland* published in 1877, a volume which, according to its author, was the 'first book on geology . . . illustrated by photographs'.

After eight successful and productive years in Leicester, Harrison gained employment as chief science master to the Birmingham School Board, and in late 1880 he moved with his wife Jane and their ten offspring from Leicester to Birmingham.

The board school system, a product of the 1870 Education Act, marked a revolutionary departure in the history of education in England. For the first time, science was recognised as an important branch of education, particularly in large manufacturing towns like Birmingham. Supported by a large staff of assistants and well-appointed laboratories at Icknield Street School, Harrison took on responsibility for 'the direction of the scientific studies of about eight thousand of the elder children, and some hundreds of the younger teachers' in Birmingham. In this capacity, he was said to have had 'as potent an influence as any man in Birmingham over the minds of the boys who will in a few years become the backbone' of the town.

In Birmingham he continued to employ photographs as visual aids in his teaching work. Using lantern slides made by professional photographers, projected through an optical lantern onto a '22-foot screen', he brought students face to face with the facts of nature in the classroom. The optical lantern soon became an indispensable aid in teaching astronomy, physics, geology, physical geography and natural history. In addition to using slides

made by other photographers, Harrison felt that it was important to 'exhibit pictures of what one had actually seen during excursions in the field', and he frequently complained that it was 'seldom indeed, that slides of the exact places or objects desired' could be purchased. It was undoubtedly, in part, his desire provide such images which led him to take up photography himself in 1881.

Twelve years after his initial appointment as chief science master, Harrison was promoted to the post of chief science demonstrator to the Birmingham School Board. He continued in this position until his death in 1908.

William Jerome Harrison was, without any doubt, a remarkable Victorian polymath. He was a geologist of national repute, an innovative educationalist, compiler of extensive bibliographies, a writer of educational books and a leading figure in the amateur photographic world of the late nineteenth century. Recognition for his contributions to numerous fields came through his election as a fellow of the Geological Society and of the British Association. He was awarded a medal by the Society of Arts in 1881; for continued work in geology he received the Darwin Medal in 1884.

Harrison's achievements were perhaps best summed up by the Rev. R. H. Coates, who, in a graveside address, declared that he:

'. . . had won for himself a distinguished position in the scientific and literary world. His singularly gifted intellect and indomitable industry had brought him growing fame in many fields, in geology,

antiquities, in chemistry and in other spheres. He was a man who not only knew how to acquire knowledge, but who also knew how to use it, and use it so as to interest and benefit others. Although he was so versed in many sciences he always took his honours modestly, considering he was but a learner still and he maintained up to the last the reverent enquiring spirit of a little child'.

W. J. Harrison FGS

A Brief Reading Guide

Harrison, W. J., 'Some Notes on a Proposed Photographic Survey of Warwickshire', *Photographic Societies Reporter*, 31 Dec. 1889, pp. 505–15.

Harrison, W. J., 'Proposal for a National Photographic Record and Survey', *Photographic News*, 8 July 1892, pp. 443–5; 29 July, pp. 484–6; 5 August p. 449; 12 August, pp. 515–17.

Harrison, W. J., *A History of Photography*, New York, Scovill Manufacturing Company, 1892.

Harrison, W. J., 'Shakespeare-Land: An Illustrated Description of Shakespeare's Country', in *The Works of William Shakespeare*, vol. xiv (The Sonnets and Poems), Eds. Sir Henry Irving and Frank A. Marshall, London, Gresham Publishing Company, 1907.

Anon. 'Mr. W. Jerome Harrison', *The Handsworth Magazine*, vol. xv, No. 169, July 1908, pp. 1–3.

James, P., 'The Evolution of the Photographic Record and Survey Movement *c.*1890–1901', *History of Photography*, July–Sept., 1988.

James, P., 'A Century of Survey Photography', *The Local Historian*, vol. 20, No. 4, Nov. 1990, pp. 166–72.

The Harrison Collection

The Harrison Collection consists of approximately 1,200 film and glass negatives of various locations in Britain taken between *c.*1888–1908: 334 of these relate specifically to Warwickshire. The Collection also contains published material, photographic journals, photographic medals, family documents, and other related ephemera. Harrison contributed just under 200 prints to the Warwickshire Photographic Survey Collection, which is housed alongside the Harrison Collection in hte Local Studies and History Service, Floor 6, Birmingham Central Library. The Library also holds copies of most of Harrison's photographic, geological, and educational publications. A full catalogue of this collection, containing a complete bibliography and details of other smaller collections is available upon request. An exhibition, 'William Jerome Harrison: Pioneer Amateur Photographer' is also available for hire.

For details phone: 021-235-4439.

The River Avon at Stratford, 1891. In the background is the parish church of Holy Trinity, where Shakespeare was baptised and where, in 1616, he was buried. The church itself, although heavily restored in 1888–92, dates mainly from the thirteenth and fourteenth centuries. The fine spire which is such a landmark was built in 1763, replacing a timber predecessor. The course of the river at Stratford was much altered by the navigation works of 1634 and by the local mills: the series of weirs was part of these changes.

Chapel Street, Stratford, in 1891. In the distance can be seen the medieval Guild Hall, rebuilt in 1417. This was the meeting place of the Guild of the Holy Cross and later of the Corporation, and had its own chapel, with a priest who was appointed by the Corporation independently of the parish church. The chapel tower and nave were rebuilt in the late fifteenth century. The building also housed the Grammar School, where Shakespeare was educated. In the nineteenth century the Guild Hall was vacated by the Corporation, and was then used as the town's fire station, but it has now been restored to its former glory. The Shakespeare Hotel, a fine half-timbered building of the late sixteenth and early seventeenth centuries, is on the left. Between it and the Guild Hall is New Place, where Shakespeare lived: this photograph shows its later Georgian front which was stripped off in 1911, revealing the original building behind; an imitation timbered front was added instead!

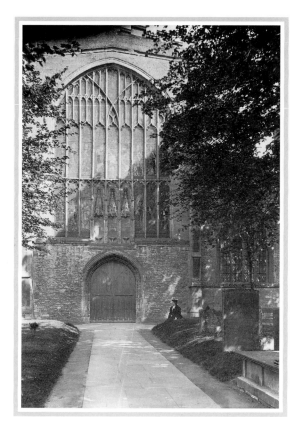

An avenue of lime trees lines the pathway from Stratford Old Town to the parish church, 1891. The great two-storeyed porch was built during the incumbency of Dean Collingwood (1491–1521), when huge windows occupying most of the wall were fashionable. Old Town and the parish church were the original village of Stratford, and dated from Saxon times: most of the later town centre was laid out in 1196 as a planned new town by Bishop John de Coutances of Worcester.

Lucy's Mill and the River Avon at Stratford. This is the site of one of Stratford's ancient water-powered cornmills – perhaps the one recorded in the Domesday Book – but the buildings shown here were built in 1819 by Thomas Lucy. They ground corn, and the river was used to transport both the grain and the flour. Warehouses were added in the 1830s and 1850s. In 1973 the mill was demolished, and replaced by a very mediocre block of flats.

Cottage at Aston Cantlow, June 1897. This detailed view of a typical Warwickshire cottage shows the timber-framing with plank boarding at the gable (often plastered over and not visible), the thick and – in this case – well-maintained thatch, and the characteristic piecemeal additions – a porch and a rainwater channel. This cottage (in fact a relatively substantial house) was probably built in the sixteenth century.

The *King's Head* at Aston Cantlow, June 1897. Aston Cantlow was called simply Estone ('the eastern settlement') in the Domesday Book: 'Cantlow' derives from the name of the Cantelupe family, who were granted the manor by King John in 1205. It is traditionally supposed that Shakespeare's parents were married at Aston Cantlow church, in 1557, although there is no contemporary record of this, and they are said to have had their wedding breakfast at the *King's Head* (although the story was not recorded until 1798!). The inn itself is beside the village green: Pevsner, the architectural historian, says in non-committal fashion that it is seventeenth- century or earlier.

Mary Arden's Cottage, Wilmcote, June 1897. The Ardens were an old Warwickshire family, but there is no contemporary evidence that Shakespeare's mother actually lived at this house, or even that it was owned by her family: this 'tradition', too, was first recorded in 1798. Robert Arden, Mary's father, did own extensive property in Wilmcote, but the family lived mainly at Snitterfield, between Stratford and Warwick. To call this a 'cottage' is highly misleading: it was in fact a very large and prosperous farmhouse, with the superb outbuildings which still survive. The building dates from the early sixteenth century, and is an outstanding example of the Midlands architecture of the period. It was well restored in the early years of this century.

The *Falcon Inn*, Bidford-on-Avon, *c.*1890. Pevsner describes the Falcon as 'A stately though irregular stone house of coursed oolite and lias [local building stones], mullioned windows. Round the corner a timber-framed part with gable and decorative lozenge patterns', and suggests that it dates from the mid sixteenth century with later additions. It stands at the end of the little market place, opposite the parish church, and by the time this picture was taken had fallen on hard times: part had been turned into the Bidford Institute and Working Men's Reading Room (1861) and the rest had been converted into seven tenements.

Mrs Baker standing in the doorway of her house, 1891. Mrs Baker's costume is typical of 'the becoming costumes of two centuries ago', which were still prevalent in rural Warwickshire in 1891. This is no ordinary house, for Mrs Baker owned Anne Hathaway's cottage in Shottery, now beautifully maintained by the Shakespeare Birthplace Trust. Although she claimed to be a descendant of the lady herself, this is very doubtful, for although William and Anne Shakespeare had three children their direct line had died out by 1670.

The village of Broom, *c.*1890. Broom features in the famous Warwickshire Village Rhyme:

Piping Pebworth, Dancing Marston / Haunted Hillboro', Hungry Grafton
Dodging Exhall, Papist Wixford / Beggarly Broom, and Drunken Bidford

The description 'Beggarly' refers to the local occupations of basket-making and knife-grinding, both of which required people to travel around the countryside, selling their wares as though beggars. This photograph illustrates vividly the way in which the 'picturesque' country cottage could be less than idyllic. It has a timber frame, raised on a brick and stone platform, and filled in with lath-and-plaster. The thatch is decaying, the plaster is falling away and disintegrating, and the brickwork of the chimney and base is in poor repair. Note the stone fence, formed of large upright slabs of lias [local limestone].

Ardens Grafton, 1891. This hamlet in Temple Grafton parish takes its name from the de Arderne family, who were granted the land by Edward I in 1292. The photograph is well composed so that the eye is led along the curving street into the picture. It shows several types of building material: there are sixteenth-century cottages with traditional timber-framing (on the left); there are houses of local lias, an attractive and high-quality building stone, the use of which became widespread at the beginning of the eighteenth century; and there are more recent brick buildings with tiled roofs.

St Mary's Church, Bearley, *c.*1890. This church has a very odd appearance and an equally confused architectural history. It was built in the late twelfth century and the chancel was added in the thirteenth or early fourteenth century. However, by the time the picture was taken there had been many alterations: in the early Victorian period the roof and upper walls, the windows, the tower and the bell turret were all rebuilt, and the nave was extended by ten feet. The result was a peculiar hotch-potch of different styles and periods: in 1961–2 the church was extensively reconstructed again.

The smithy at Dorsington, 1895. The tiny village of Dorsington, south-west of Stratford, belonged to Gloucestershire until boundary changes in 1931 transferred it to Warwickshire. The smithy shown here was built of stone, with a tiled roof and boarded gables, and was probably erected in the late eighteenth century. It was tacked on to the side of a much older thatched timber-framed cottage. The buildings are beautifully maintained: note the neat piles of brushwood to the right of the smithy – perhaps to be used for fences and hurdles.

Farmhouse and barn at Dorsington, 1895. The village consists of a few farms and cottages (including Moat House Farm where there are remains of the moat) and an eighteenth-century church on the site of an older chapel, all built around a small green. In the 1890s the buildings shown here were in a state of disrepair – a feature which will be seen in many of these pictures. The house is dilapidated, the ivy is rampant, the outbuildings are ramshackle and there is no garden to speak of. The immaculate country cottages which we associate with rural England are often the product of the taste and money of our own century.

Harrison was internationally recognised as one of this country's leading geologists: he was responsible for the county-by-county geological surveys of the British Isles which appeared in Kelly's Directories, and published other reports and studies. His researches into the geology of Warwickshire and adjacent counties combined well with the photography: here (1895) he shows a large boulder of volcanic ash at Exhall near Coventry. It is an erratic, a stray piece of rock from the north of England or Scotland carried by an ice-sheet during the last Ice Age and dumped in what was later to be Warwickshire as the ice melted.

St Giles' Church, Exhall, near Alcester, *c*.1895. The church has a Norman nave, much altered, and a most unusual square-topped window of *c*.1320. The bellcote was built in 1862, during a comprehensive 'restoration', which involved the removal of a fine Norman doorway, the old windows, a medieval bell turret and other ancient work, despite the fierce protests of the Worcester Diocesan Archaeological Society. The contrast between old and new work can be seen in the picture. Note the hay-making in progress on the village green.

Ryknield Street, near Studley, *c.*1891. This was one of the three Roman roads which crossed Warwickshire: it ran from Bidford, via Alcester, towards Birmingham. The houses shown were built in the 1840s, as estate cottages for the Studley Castle estate. The castle itself had been rebuilt in an extravagant Gothic style after 1834 for the new lord of the manor, Sir Francis Goodricke, and these cottages, with their tall chimneys, 'Gothic' gables and neat brickwork reflect the contemporary enthusiasm for 'model' agricultural dwellings.

Luddington, *c.*1895. The village stands beside the Avon, just below Stratford, and it was sweepingly dismissed by W. H. Hutton in his book *Highways and Byways in Shakespeare's Country* (1914): 'There is no need to visit Luddington as there is nothing there'. Harrison's photograph shows that he was wrong – but perhaps quaint thatched cottages were considered too commonplace in Edwardian Warwickshire to merit special attention.

The ancient chapel of Luddington, where William Shakespeare and Anne Hathaway are thought to have been married, was demolished in the nineteenth century – though traces of the foundations can still be seen. The font was taken away and left in the open air by the roadside, where Harrison photographed it in about 1895: his daughter Margaret gives the scale. A new church was built to designs by John Cotton in 1871, and the old font has now been rescued and placed in the present building.

The River Avon at Luddington, *c.*1895. Below Stratford the Avon meanders lazily through the meadows. Harrison particularly liked the river, and in his book *Shakespeare Land*, an illustrated description of Warwickshire, he paints an evocative and charming word-picture: 'In summer its surface is here and there completely covered with the small white flowers of the water crowfoot; forests of bulrushes crowd its banks; and the yellow water lily, the bitter cress, and the water meadow grass grow profusely'.

The church of St James, Long Marston, *c*.1895. Long Marston, at the southern end of the county, justifies its name: 'Marston' means 'marshy place', and the damp meadows of the Avon floodplain were indeed marshy a thousand years ago. And the village is strung out for almost a mile along its single main street. The church, described by Pevsner as 'pretty . . . with its timber-framed bell-turret', has a medieval nave and chancel, but the turret is a Victorian reconstruction.

The dovecote at Hillborough Manor, *c.*1898. This dovecote, one of several splendid examples in Warwickshire, is twenty-four feet in diameter and built of stone, with walls a yard thick to hold the nesting spaces for 900 pairs of pigeons. Hillborough Manor is almost all that is left in a deserted medieval village – there were only two farms here as long ago as 1730. The house itself dates from the sixteenth and eighteenth centuries, and it has a very good group of eighteenth-century farm buildings: the dovecote probably dates from this time, too.

Temple Grafton, *c.*1895. In this idyllic scene, the little girls in their large sun bonnets conjure up memories or imaginary pictures of warm summers long gone. To their right is a water pump, an essential feature of village life in the days before piped water supplies, though many people in the 1890s still used streams and old-fashioned wells. The cottages shown here, although thatched in the traditional style, are built of brick, and were probably erected in the late eighteenth century.

Temple Grafton, *c.*1895. The village owes its name to the Knights Templar, who built a church here. The village underwent major changes after the purchase of the manor by James Carlisle in 1862. He pulled down the medieval church and manor house, built a new church, rectory and village school, and constructed a replacement manor house, called Temple Grafton Court. However, the houses shown here had escaped his improving hand: the one on the left, built of timber and plaster, is probably sixteenth-century in date; that on the right, brick with a tiled roof, is likely to be a century or so later. Note the local 'everyday' costumes, with shawl, apron and large coif bonnet – and the baby wrapped in a thick knitted woollen blanket.

The village of Wixford, *c*.1890. In the Village Rhyme this was 'Papist Wixford': the Throckmorton family of Coughton Court, one of the few prominent Roman Catholic families in the county, were lords of the manor. They bought the manor in 1562 and held it until 1696, then repurchased in 1776, after which they kept it until forced to sell up in 1919. The view of the village street shows typical features of many country villages: a rough, rutted and unmade road, raised sidewalks, a tumbledown fence and small children larking around!

Cottages at Binton, June 1897. Binton, on the edge of the Cotswold stone belt, has warm golden stone which gives an air of tranquillity and permanence to its buildings. There were important stone quarries here, operating until about the time this picture was taken. Even here, though, the influence of the industrial age is apparent in the use of brick for the house to the left of the picture – its patterned brick front looks out of place here, although it would have been at home on the edge of one of Warwickshire's great industrial towns.

Charlecote, *c.*1890. The house at Charlecote was built between 1551 and 1558 for Thomas Lucy – the property had been in his family since at least the twelfth century. In about 1583 Shakespeare is said to have been caught poaching Sir Thomas' deer in Charlecote Park, and to have fled to London in consequence – the rest being history … There is some evidence to suggest that Shakespeare did not like Sir Thomas: he was the model for Justice Shallow in *The Merry Wives of Windsor.* On the arms of the Lucy family were three luces (pike), and Justice Shallow sported 'the dozen white luces on his coat [of arms]'.

The wheelwright of Balsall Street. This magnificent photograph was one of five taken by Harrison on 17 May 1890. The wheelwright was Richard Holmes Thompson, described by Harrison as 'a typical Warwickshire man of the present day'.

The wheelwright's shop, Balsall Street. Here Richard Thompson is seen at work, a scene which must have been characteristic of almost every large village in late nineteenth century England, but one which has now completely vanished. The primitive conditions in which the business was conducted are vividly portrayed: a crude wooden shed with a thatched roof, untidy piles of spare timber, everything made painstakingly and carefully by hand – 'progress' has swept such scenes away.

The church of St John, Berkswell, 1890. According to Pevsner this is 'easily the most interesting Norman village church in Warwickshire'. It has much surviving Norman and twelfth-century work, and an impressive crypt which may be adapted from an Anglo-Saxon original (though nobody is at all sure). The extraordinary two-storey half-timbered porch, with an outside staircase, is probably fifteenth-century – it is cut into a Norman doorway. The old man is, once again, Richard Dingle, a retired farmer who lived at the almshouses on the green, and who makes an appearance in many photographs of the village in the 1890s.

The stocks at Berkswell near Coventry, 1890. The village, one of the prettiest in the Arden district of mid-Warwickshire, derives its name from the well, the strong spring which rises close to the churchyard and feeds a great stone tank, sixteen feet square. On the green are the stocks, the subject of several legends because they have five leg holes (a one-legged thief is one explanation!). The charming cottages behind have now been replaced by estate bungalows, while to the right are the brick-built almshouses of 1853. The old man is a celebrated local character, Richard Dingle.

The Manor House, Hampton-in-Arden, 1891. This apparently ancient building, irregular and gabled, was in fact built in 1870–3 for Sir Frederick Peel, the son of the great Prime Minister Sir Robert Peel. It was designed by Eden Nesfield in a remarkable and successful exercise in antiquarianism – the house seems ancient, and the impression is wholly convincing. The countryside around Hampton-in-Arden has been bruised and battered by motorways, the airport and other signs of the late twentieth century, but the village itself has survived unexpectedly well.

Tanworth-in-Arden, *c.*1895. Tanworth, like Hampton, derives its name from the great Forest of Arden which covered most of central Warwickshire and which, of course, had a significant influence upon Shakespeare. The church, built in the early fourteenth century, dominates the funnel-shaped main street. The church is an architectural puzzle: although it was apparently built all at the same time, there are odd features which do not conform with the rest of the building, and the chancel is markedly out of alignment. Pevsner wonders whether it was designed and built by people who were not too talented at their job!

Tanworth-in-Arden village, *c.*1895. Here, as in other pictures in this book, the muddy unmade village streets of the 1890s are very clear. The houses show a typical mixture of timber-framing and brick, with steps to some of the front doors. Tanworth is set on a hilltop with wide views, and its relative remoteness from main roads and railways protected it from development as the influence of Birmingham began to affect neighbouring communities. More recently it has been 'zealously guarded by its Village Preservation Society'. Its character remains remarkably unchanged.

The River Blythe at Temple Balsall, 1895. The name Blythe means 'peaceful' or 'calm', and this seems a particularly apt description for this scene, with the willows growing tall beside the quiet waters of the river. The view was taken at the old ford just east of the tiny village of Temple Balsall. The river flows into the murky waters of the Tame at Blyth End near Coleshill.

High Street, Knowle village, *c.*1892. Today Knowle High Street, though still lined by attractive buildings, suffers from constant heavy traffic. In 1892 life was a great deal quieter – though doubtless the picturesque cottages were less sanitary and clean than they are today. Although it is so near Birmingham, and has been greatly expanded since 1945, Knowle retains its village character, with seventeenth-century timber-framed cottages and eighteenth-century brick houses.

The *White Swan* at Knowle, 1891. The *White Swan* was a building of very great historical and architectural interest. It dated from the late fifteenth century, and consisted of an almost unaltered medieval hall block in the centre (the lower part of the building) with timber-framed cross-wings at either end – the classic design for a small medieval manor house. As an inn it was at the centre of much of the life of the village, and famous for its magnificent iron sign projecting across the street. Derelict and uncared-for by the late 1930s, this precious building was pulled down after the war, and only the sign, now gracing the nearby seventeenth-century *Red Lion*, survives.

Chamberlain Place, Birmingham, 1892. Now renamed Chamberlain Square, this commemorates one of Birmingham's most famous adopted sons, Joseph Chamberlain. He revolutionised English local government, developing effective and efficient municipal enterprise into a commercial success and an object of civic pride, and seeing local government as something truly worthy and honourable. During his time as the Mayor of Birmingham (1873–6) he oversaw the repaving of the city's streets, the purchase of the private gas company by the corporation (followed by the doubling of its annual profits and a drastic reduction in the price paid by consumers), and major improvement in the water supplies. The fountain was erected in 1880 to mark his period as mayor. In the background is the superb Council House and Art Gallery of 1874–9.

The Crown Inn, Deritend, 1892. This is one of Birmingham's oldest buildings, which survived comparatively unscathed while most of the city's medieval and sixteenth-century architecture was swept away. Although supposedly built in 1368, it is in fact a typical substantial mid sixteenth-century timber-framed house. It was threatened with demolition on several occasions because of poor repair or because it lay in the path of proposed roads. In 1934 it was purchased by Holt's Brewery and became a public house once more – renamed *The Old Crown*.

Horse-bus in Monument Road, Birmingham, *c.*1895. This is an enlarged detail from one of Harrison's photographs, and shows a scene which was characteristic of the city's suburbs late in the Victorian period. On either side of the street are mid nineteenth-century terraced properties, substantial and – when they were built – fashionable residences. The horse-bus is significant. This was a relatively prosperous district, and no tramways had yet reached it, so a horse-bus (a genteel form of commuting) served.

The Plough and Harrow Hotel, Hagley Road, Birmingham, *c.*1895. This hotel was built in the early nineteenth century, just as the fashion for Gothic architecture was replacing the Georgian tradition. Its remarkable (and purely decorative) sharply-pointed gables are very distinctive, as are the tall 'Jacobean' chimneys. The hotel still retains much of its Victorian character.

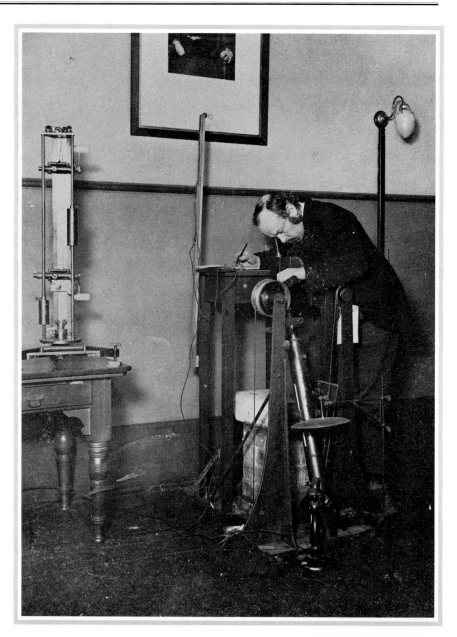

Professor Poynting weighing the Earth at Mason's College in 1892. Professor J. H. Poynting was a friend of Harrison, born in Manchester in 1852. At the time this picture was taken he was one of the most distinguished members of the teaching staff at the new University of Birmingham. He calculated the weight of the Earth at 1.25×10^{21} pounds. In fact it is much heavier, the weight (or more properly mass) of the Earth is now believed to be 5.974×10^{21} tonnes, equivalent to about 2.845×10^{25} pounds.

The laboratory at Icknield Street School, Birmingham, c.1896. Harrison was brought from Leicester to teach science in the Birmingham board schools – he was one of the pioneers of science education in schools. He believed firmly not only that schools should teach scientific subjects, but that the lessons should be practical and interesting. He therefore devised a travelling kit, mounted on a handcart, which he could take to schools to use for demonstrating scientific experiments. He also made use of magic lantern slides to stimulate his pupils' interest.

Butcher Row, Coventry, *c.*1895. Until the tragedy of 1940 Coventry was one of the finest of English medieval cities, with a wealth of timber-framed buildings. However, some of the oldest areas had been swept away even before the war. In the area of the old Bull Ring, where the butchers had had their stalls (the traditional 'Shambles') were several streets and lanes of medieval and sixteenth-century buildings which were cleared for the construction of Trinity Street in 1935–7. Butcher Row was one of these.

Ford's, or Greyfriars, Hospital, Coventry, 1895. Ford's Hospital was built in about 1510–12, under the terms of the will of William Ford, a Coventry cloth and wool merchant. He left money to endow a hospital (a term which then meant a refuge or sanctuary) for five elderly and deserving men and five women. The building has three end gables onto Greyfriars Lane, and inside there is a long narrow courtyard.

Swanswell Gate, *c.*1905; sometimes known as Priory Gate, this is one of only two surviving out of the original twelve gates in Coventry City wall. The photograph can be dated by the advertising hoarding for the proposed Hippodrome in nearby Hales Street, which was opened on 31 December 1906. The appearance of the area has changed a great deal since the photograph was taken. All of the surrounding buildings have been demolished, and the pitched roof of the gate itself has been replaced by a flat one.

The courtyard of Ford's Hospital, 1895. The hospital was noted for its very fine elaborately carved bargeboards, clearly seen in this view. In 1940 it was devastated during the Coventry air raids, but in the early 1950s a meticulous restoration and reconstruction was carried out, making extensive use of contemporary early sixteenth-century timbers salvaged from other bomb-wrecked buildings in the city. The result was a triumph – the building today is scarcely distinguishable from that shown in Harrison's photographs.

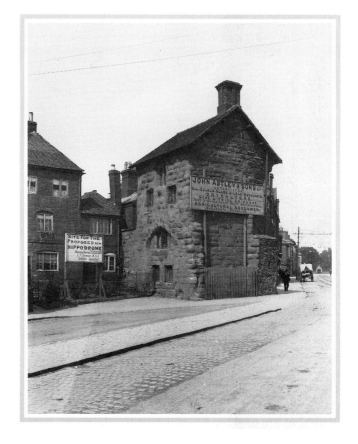

Kenilworth Castle, 1890. The ruins of Kenilworth Castle have long been admired for their architectural and historical importance, and for their dramatic and romantic visual impact. The castle was built around a mighty Norman keep, but in the later medieval period a series of comfortable apartments and domestic buildings was constructed. In the 1560s Robert Dudley, Earl of Leicester, the favourite of Elizabeth I, lived at Kenilworth and undertook further building, some of it to honour the presence of the Queen herself when she came here on progresses. The castle was destroyed, and its great moats drained, after the Civil War.

Guy's Cliffe House, 1898. This extraordinary assemblage of buildings began, in the fourteenth century, with the hermit's cave cut into the cliff above the Avon. A chapel was added in 1422. The place was an object of pilgrimage because of the hermits, and legends about the saintly Saxon hermit, Guy of Warwick, brought added interest. In 1751 a classical mansion was built, incorporating some of the early buildings, and this was given a Gothic façade in the early nineteenth century. The house is now a gaunt and bizarre ruin, thickly overgrown with trees, although the chapel is still intact.

Guy's Cliffe Mill, *c.*1891. According to Dugdale, there was a mill at Guy's Cliffe before the Norman Conquest, but the building seen here was built in 1822: it probably incorporates parts of older buildings, but its ornate 'Gothick' timberwork is characteristic of the antiquarian fancies of the Regency period. The mill was in use, grinding corn, until the Second World War, and has now been converted into a restaurant. Nearby is a seventeenth-century timber and stone mill house.

Lillington, *c.*1895. The old village of Lillington is now swamped by the suburban housing estates of Leamington: it was annexed by the town in 1890. St Mary's Church, next to what was once the village green, has a fourteenth-century chancel and tower, but the remainder was rebuilt between 1847 and 1884. The great oak tree nearby was said, like several other places in Warwickshire, to mark the geographical centre of England.

Bishops Tachbrook, 1895. Bishops Tachbrook has so far escaped being overwhelmed by Leamington, although the suburbs of the town are creeping ever closer, and there is much new housing in the village. The church of St Chad is partly Norman, with some later medieval work, but – as with so many Warwickshire village churches – much of what is seen is actually a Victorian rebuilding.

Barford, 1890. Barford, a picturesque village on the banks of the Avon south west of Warwick, now suffers from the problem of heavy through traffic, but that was not thought of in 1890! It was the birthplace of the great agricultural trade union leader Joseph Arch, the first farm labourer to become an M.P. In this view there is more evidence of the sad disrepair of many of the old buildings in Warwickshire villages in Harrison's time: note, too, that the thatch on one of the cottages has been replaced by tiling – a sign of the times, since tiles, though less quaint, were a great deal cheaper and easier to maintain.

Cottages at Harbury, *c.*1895. This village, just south of Southam, was long known as 'Hungry Harbury' because of its soil, less fertile and more difficult to work than in other parts of the county. Nevertheless, it has some fine sixteenth- and seventeenth- century houses. These cottages, with their complex deep gables and thick thatch, look extremely attractive – but here, too, the plaster is peeling and falling away. The paling fences are characteristic of Warwickshire villages at this period.

The Grammar School, Chilvers Coton, 1895. Chilvers Coton, near Nuneaton, is best known perhaps for Arbury Farm, the birthplace of George Eliot. The Free Grammar School was founded by the lady of the manor, Lady Newdigate, in 1745. The severely classical buildings, perfectly symmetrical in plan and elevation, were erected by her son, Sir Roger Newdigate, in the 1790s.

Caldecote windmill near Nuneaton, 1895. This very impressive tower mill, with mixed common and patent sails, ogee cap and fantail gear mechanism, has long been demolished. In 1895, when John Henry Morris was the miller, it was one of many which dotted the Warwickshire countryside: of the three hundred or more windmills known to have been built in Warwickshire since the early thirteenth century there were fewer than fifty left in Harrison's day.

The old Norman chapel at Dosthill, Kingsbury, 1895. The very plain, barn-like Norman chapel at Dosthill, a very good example of the most basic post-Conquest ecclesiastical architecture, was replaced by a new church, dedicated to St Paul and designed by Holmes of Birmingham, in 1870–2. The old chapel was then used as a church hall, which was its role when Harrison visited in 1895.

Sheep drovers at Griff, near Nuneaton, 1895. Another typical Warwickshire scene which is now a rarity – and certainly at Griff: the street shown here is now the main road between Nuneaton and Bedworth! Sheep-farming was at one time a major occupation in Warwickshire, and the desertion and depopulation of many of the medieval villages in the county was in part due to the creation of great sheep farms. Griff was itself such a depopulated village, until it began to grow again in the late nineteenth century.

Narrowboats on the Coventry Canal, Nuneaton, 1895. The extension of the canal to Nuneaton in 1771 allowed locally mined coal to be shipped cheaply to the lucrative markets of Oxford, the Thames Valley and London. The North Warwickshire coalfield expanded rapidly in consequence, while the great stone quarries at Hartshill also benefited from the improved transport links. Here tramway wagons are seen unloading coal into narrowboats using chutes.

Bridge Street, Nuneaton, *c.*1895. Until the twelfth century the town was simply called Eaton, but the foundation of a convent in 1155 led to the addition of the word 'Nun'. The ancient market town has been much altered by industrialisation since 1800. Here we see the old Bull Hotel – now renamed the George Eliot in honour of the town's most celebrated product. The plain and rather severe Georgian building was Nuneaton's first Post Office: the London mail coaches arrived and departed from the Bull between 1792 and the 1850s, and the innkeeper doubled as the postmaster.

Maxstoke Priory, 1892. The priory was founded in 1336 as a house of Augustinian canons by Sir William de Clinton, who also built the nearby castle. At the Dissolution it was purchased by Charles Brandon, Duke of Suffolk, and then passed to a long series of different owners. The fabric was largely destroyed and the stonework sold, so that by the 1890s only a few ruined walls and the ivy-grown crossing tower remained. Since then even more has gone: the tower, neglected and uncared-for, collapsed in 1988.

Coleshill from the river, 1892. Coleshill is a very ancient market centre, and its splendid church spire is a landmark for miles around. The bypass, built in the 1930s, has protected the town from at least some of the damage which might have resulted from its position on a main trunk road, and many sixteenth- to eighteenth-century buildings survive. The eighteenth-century St Paul's house is seen here behind the very fine sixteenth-century bridge over the River Cole.

A newly uncovered geological fault line, 1899. Harrison, as an active and enthusiastic geologist, was always on the look-out for new discoveries. In 1899 workmen excavating a cutting on a new mineral railway at Chapel End, Nuneaton, exposed a very clear geological fault line, and Harrison went to investigate. Here the fault can be seen on the side of the cutting, marked by the two long-handled hammers (the hammer heads are approximately on the line of the fault).

Coleshill pillory and whipping post, *c*.1890. The pillory, whipping post, stocks and manacles at Coleshill are among the best remaining examples in Britain – once such reminders of summary justice were a commonplace sight up and down the country. The pillory formerly stood in front of the old market hall on Church Hill, but in 1863 was moved to its present site in front of the Institute building. Just before the move the stocks were used for the last time, to punish two drunken labourers.